EMMANUEL JOSEPH

The Wellness Renaissance, A Journey through Health, Wealth, and Interpersonal Enlightenment

Copyright © 2025 by Emmanuel Joseph

All rights reserved. No part of this publication may be reproduced, stored or transmitted in any form or by any means, electronic, mechanical, photocopying, recording, scanning, or otherwise without written permission from the publisher. It is illegal to copy this book, post it to a website, or distribute it by any other means without permission.

First edition

This book was professionally typeset on Reedsy.
Find out more at reedsy.com

Contents

1	Chapter 1: The Awakening	1
2	Chapter 2: The Foundation of Health	3
3	Chapter 3: Nourishing the Body	5
4	Chapter 4: The Power of Movement	7
5	Chapter 5: Rest and Recovery	8
6	Chapter 6: Financial Wellness	9
7	Chapter 7: Building Wealth	11
8	Chapter 8: Sustainable Wealth	13
9	Chapter 9: Interpersonal Connections	15
10	Chapter 10: Emotional Intelligence	17
11	Chapter 11: The Power of Connection	19
12	Chapter 12: Mindful Communication	21
13	Chapter 13: Cultivating Gratitude	23
14	Chapter 14: The Path to Enlightenment	25
15	Chapter 15: Embracing the Wellness Renaissance	27

1

Chapter 1: The Awakening

In the modern world, the pursuit of wellness has evolved into a holistic journey that encompasses physical health, financial stability, and meaningful relationships. This journey, known as the Wellness Renaissance, marks a transformative era where individuals seek a balanced and fulfilling life. The chapter introduces this concept, highlighting the interconnectedness of health, wealth, and interpersonal enlightenment. By embracing these elements, we can achieve a higher state of well-being and navigate the complexities of contemporary life with ease and grace.

The journey begins with a shift in mindset—a conscious decision to prioritize wellness in all aspects of life. This awakening is not merely about adopting healthy habits, but about cultivating a deeper understanding of oneself and the world around us. It involves recognizing the significance of physical health, financial freedom, and the strength of our relationships. The chapter emphasizes the importance of self-awareness and personal growth as foundational elements of the Wellness Renaissance.

As we embark on this journey, it is essential to acknowledge the challenges and obstacles that may arise. The path to wellness is not always linear, and setbacks are a natural part of the process. However, by maintaining a positive attitude and staying committed to our goals, we can overcome these challenges and continue to grow. The chapter explores the role of resilience and perseverance in achieving wellness, encouraging readers to embrace the journey with an open heart and mind.

The Wellness Renaissance is not a solitary endeavor—it is a collective movement that thrives on community and support. By connecting with others who share similar goals and values, we can create a network of encouragement and accountability. The chapter highlights the importance of building and nurturing relationships that inspire and uplift us. Together, we can navigate the wellness journey and contribute to a more enlightened and harmonious world.

2

Chapter 2: The Foundation of Health

Health is the cornerstone of a vibrant and fulfilling life. It is the bedrock upon which all other aspects of wellness are built. This chapter delves into the essential pillars of physical well-being, emphasizing the importance of nutrition, exercise, and sleep. By understanding and prioritizing these elements, we can lay a strong foundation for overall health.

Nutrition is the fuel that powers our bodies. A balanced diet, rich in whole foods, provides the necessary nutrients for optimal functioning. This chapter explores the principles of healthy eating, including the benefits of consuming a variety of fruits, vegetables, lean proteins, and whole grains. It also discusses the dangers of processed foods and the impact of poor dietary choices on long-term health. Practical tips for making healthier food choices and developing a sustainable eating plan are provided.

Exercise is another critical component of physical health. Regular physical activity not only helps maintain a healthy weight but also improves cardiovascular health, strengthens muscles, and enhances mental well-being. This chapter examines the benefits of different types of exercise, such as cardiovascular workouts, strength training, and flexibility exercises. It offers guidance on creating a personalized fitness routine that fits individual preferences and lifestyles. The chapter also discusses strategies for staying motivated and incorporating movement into daily life.

Sleep and recovery are often overlooked but are crucial for overall well-being. Quality sleep is essential for physical and mental restoration, while relaxation practices help manage stress and promote balance. This chapter delves into the science of sleep, the consequences of sleep deprivation, and techniques for improving sleep quality. It also explores various relaxation methods, such as meditation, deep breathing exercises, and mindfulness practices. By prioritizing rest and recovery, we can support our body's natural healing processes and enhance our overall health.

3

Chapter 3: Nourishing the Body

Proper nutrition is the key to a healthy and vibrant life. This chapter delves deeper into the principles of a balanced diet and the benefits of nourishing the body with wholesome foods. It emphasizes the importance of mindful eating and developing a positive relationship with food.

Whole foods, such as fruits, vegetables, whole grains, lean proteins, and healthy fats, provide essential nutrients that support bodily functions and prevent chronic diseases. This chapter discusses the nutritional value of these foods and offers practical tips for incorporating them into daily meals. It also highlights the dangers of processed foods, which are often high in sugar, salt, and unhealthy fats, and their negative impact on health.

Different dietary approaches, such as plant-based eating, intermittent fasting, and the Mediterranean diet, offer various benefits for health and wellness. This chapter explores these approaches, discussing their principles, benefits, and potential challenges. It provides guidance on choosing a dietary plan that aligns with individual health goals and preferences.

Mindful eating is about being present and fully engaged during meals. It involves paying attention to hunger and fullness cues, savoring each bite, and appreciating the sensory experience of eating. This chapter offers strategies for practicing mindful eating, such as eating slowly, avoiding distractions, and tuning into the body's signals. By developing a healthy relationship with food, we can enjoy the act of eating while nourishing our bodies.

4

Chapter 4: The Power of Movement

Physical activity is essential for maintaining health and vitality. This chapter explores the benefits of regular exercise and offers practical tips for incorporating movement into daily life.

Exercise improves cardiovascular health, strengthens muscles and bones, enhances flexibility, and boosts mental well-being. This chapter discusses the benefits of various types of exercise, such as aerobic workouts, strength training, and flexibility exercises. It provides guidance on creating a personalized fitness routine that fits individual preferences and goals.

Staying motivated to exercise can be challenging, but it is crucial for maintaining a consistent fitness routine. This chapter offers strategies for staying motivated, such as setting realistic goals, tracking progress, and finding activities that are enjoyable. It also discusses the importance of variety in an exercise routine to prevent boredom and promote overall fitness.

Incorporating movement into daily life goes beyond structured workouts. This chapter provides tips for staying active throughout the day, such as taking the stairs instead of the elevator, walking or biking instead of driving, and doing household chores with enthusiasm. By making movement a natural part of daily life, we can reap the benefits of physical activity and support overall health.

5

Chapter 5: Rest and Recovery

Sleep and relaxation are crucial for overall well-being. This chapter examines the science of sleep and relaxation, offering strategies for improving sleep quality and incorporating relaxation practices into daily life.

Quality sleep is essential for physical and mental restoration. This chapter explores the stages of sleep, the role of the circadian rhythm, and the impact of sleep deprivation on health. It offers practical tips for improving sleep hygiene, such as maintaining a consistent sleep schedule, creating a relaxing bedtime routine, and optimizing the sleep environment.

Relaxation practices, such as meditation, deep breathing exercises, and mindfulness, help manage stress and promote balance. This chapter discusses the benefits of these practices and provides guidance on incorporating them into daily life. It also explores other relaxation techniques, such as yoga, progressive muscle relaxation, and visualization, offering a variety of options for finding relaxation and inner peace.

Prioritizing rest and recovery is essential for supporting the body's natural healing processes and enhancing overall well-being. This chapter emphasizes the importance of making time for relaxation and self-care, encouraging readers to listen to their bodies and honor their need for rest.

6

Chapter 6: Financial Wellness

F inancial wellness is more than just having money; it's about achieving financial freedom and security. This chapter delves into the importance of financial literacy and provides practical tips for managing personal finances. By understanding and implementing sound financial principles, we can create a stable foundation for our overall well-being.

Financial literacy is the ability to understand and effectively manage financial resources. This chapter covers essential financial concepts, such as budgeting, saving, investing, and debt management. It emphasizes the importance of creating a budget to track income and expenses, setting financial goals, and building an emergency fund. Practical tips for reducing debt and improving credit scores are also provided.

Saving and investing are crucial for building wealth and achieving financial security. This chapter discusses the benefits of saving regularly, the power of compound interest, and the importance of diversifying investments. It offers guidance on different investment options, such as stocks, bonds, mutual funds, and real estate. The chapter also explores the role of retirement planning and provides tips for creating a retirement savings plan.

Debt management is a critical aspect of financial wellness. This chapter examines the impact of debt on overall well-being and offers strategies for managing and reducing debt. It discusses the importance of understanding different types of debt, such as credit card debt, student loans, and mortgages. Practical tips for negotiating with creditors, consolidating debt, and avoiding future debt are provided.

7

Chapter 7: Building Wealth

Creating wealth requires a strategic approach and a strong mindset. This chapter delves into the principles of wealth-building, including entrepreneurship, passive income, and smart investments. It offers insights into identifying opportunities and mitigating risks, providing a roadmap for achieving financial success.

Entrepreneurship is a powerful way to create wealth and achieve financial independence. This chapter explores the benefits of starting a business, the challenges entrepreneurs face, and the key steps to launching a successful venture. It discusses the importance of market research, business planning, and networking. Practical tips for finding funding, building a brand, and scaling a business are provided.

Passive income is another essential component of wealth-building. This chapter discusses different sources of passive income, such as rental properties, dividend stocks, and royalties. It offers guidance on identifying and evaluating passive income opportunities, creating multiple streams of income, and leveraging assets to generate revenue. The chapter emphasizes the importance of creating a diversified portfolio to reduce risk and increase financial stability.

Smart investments are crucial for growing wealth and achieving long-term financial goals. This chapter explores various investment strategies, such as value investing, growth investing, and index investing. It discusses the importance of conducting thorough research, understanding market trends, and managing risk. Practical tips for building and maintaining a diversified investment portfolio are provided.

8

Chapter 8: Sustainable Wealth

Wealth should be built and maintained with sustainability in mind. This chapter explores the concept of sustainable investing, ethical consumption, and the role of philanthropy in financial wellness. By aligning financial goals with personal values, we can create a positive impact on society and achieve long-term financial success.

Sustainable investing involves choosing investments that promote environmental, social, and governance (ESG) criteria. This chapter discusses the benefits of sustainable investing, the principles of ESG investing, and the different types of sustainable investment options. It provides guidance on evaluating ESG factors, selecting sustainable investments, and building a portfolio that aligns with personal values.

Ethical consumption is about making conscious choices that promote social and environmental responsibility. This chapter explores the importance of supporting ethical businesses, reducing consumption, and choosing sustainable products. It offers practical tips for becoming a more conscious consumer, such as researching companies, prioritizing quality over quantity, and minimizing waste.

Philanthropy plays a vital role in financial wellness and personal fulfillment. This chapter discusses the benefits of charitable giving, the different ways to give, and the impact of philanthropy on society. It provides guidance on choosing causes to support, creating a giving plan, and making a difference through volunteer work. The chapter emphasizes the importance of giving back and contributing to a better world.

9

Chapter 9: Interpersonal Connections

Healthy relationships are a key component of overall well-being. This chapter discusses the importance of building and maintaining strong interpersonal connections. By fostering meaningful relationships, we can enhance our mental and emotional health and create a supportive network.

Communication is the foundation of healthy relationships. This chapter explores the principles of effective communication, including active listening, empathy, and assertiveness. It provides practical tips for improving communication skills, resolving conflicts, and building trust. The chapter also discusses the impact of nonverbal communication and the importance of being present in interactions.

Empathy is the ability to understand and share the feelings of others. This chapter delves into the role of empathy in building strong relationships, fostering connection, and promoting emotional well-being. It offers strategies for developing empathy, such as practicing active listening, putting oneself in others' shoes, and responding with compassion. The chapter emphasizes the importance of empathy in creating meaningful connections.

Conflict resolution is essential for maintaining healthy relationships. This chapter examines the common causes of conflict, the impact of unresolved conflict on relationships, and the principles of effective conflict resolution. It provides practical tips for addressing conflicts, finding common ground, and creating win-win solutions. The chapter also discusses the importance of forgiveness and letting go of grudges.

10

Chapter 10: Emotional Intelligence

Emotional intelligence is crucial for navigating relationships and achieving personal growth. This chapter delves into the components of emotional intelligence, including self-awareness, self-regulation, motivation, empathy, and social skills. By developing emotional intelligence, we can enhance our relationships and achieve interpersonal enlightenment.

Self-awareness is the ability to recognize and understand our own emotions, strengths, and weaknesses. This chapter discusses the importance of self-awareness in personal growth and relationship building. It offers strategies for developing self-awareness, such as journaling, seeking feedback, and practicing mindfulness. The chapter emphasizes the role of self-reflection in achieving emotional intelligence.

Self-regulation involves managing our emotions and reactions in a healthy and constructive way. This chapter explores the principles of self-regulation, including stress management, impulse control, and emotional resilience. It provides practical tips for developing self-regulation skills, such as practicing relaxation techniques, setting boundaries, and cultivating a positive mindset. The chapter highlights the importance of self-regulation in achieving emotional balance.

Motivation is the drive to achieve goals and pursue personal growth. This chapter delves into the role of motivation in emotional intelligence and provides strategies for staying motivated, setting goals, and maintaining focus.

It discusses the importance of intrinsic motivation and finding purpose in one's pursuits. The chapter offers practical tips for overcoming obstacles and staying committed to personal growth.

11

Chapter 11: The Power of Connection

Human beings are inherently social creatures, and connection is essential for well-being. This chapter explores the science of human connection and the impact of social isolation on health. By building and maintaining social networks, we can enhance our overall wellness and create a sense of belonging.

Connection is a fundamental human need. This chapter discusses the importance of social support, the benefits of close relationships, and the impact of loneliness on health. It provides insights into the various ways connection influences physical and mental well-being, including reducing stress, boosting immune function, and increasing life satisfaction.

Building and maintaining social networks requires effort and intentionality. This chapter offers strategies for fostering connections, such as joining social groups, volunteering, and participating in community activities. It discusses the role of technology in facilitating connections, offering tips for using social media and online platforms to stay connected. The chapter also highlights the importance of nurturing existing relationships and making time for loved ones.

Community plays a vital role in our sense of connection. This chapter explores the benefits of being part of a community, such as increased support, shared resources, and a sense of belonging. It provides guidance on finding and engaging with communities that align with personal values and interests.

The chapter emphasizes the importance of contributing to the community and creating a positive impact.

12

Chapter 12: Mindful Communication

Effective communication is the foundation of healthy relationships. This chapter discusses the principles of mindful communication, including active listening, nonviolent communication, and assertiveness. By improving communication skills, we can enhance our relationships and achieve interpersonal enlightenment.

Active listening involves fully engaging with the speaker, paying attention to their words, and responding with empathy. This chapter explores the benefits of active listening, such as building trust, fostering connection, and resolving conflicts. It offers practical tips for practicing active listening, such as making eye contact, avoiding interruptions, and reflecting back what the speaker has said.

Nonviolent communication is a method of expressing oneself honestly and empathetically while maintaining respect for others. This chapter delves into the principles of nonviolent communication, including observing without judgment, expressing feelings and needs, and making requests. It provides guidance on using nonviolent communication to resolve conflicts and build understanding. The chapter emphasizes the importance of empathy and compassion in communication.

Assertiveness is the ability to express oneself confidently and respectfully. This chapter discusses the benefits of assertiveness, such as increased self-esteem, improved relationships, and reduced stress. It offers practical tips for developing assertiveness skills, such as setting boundaries, using "I" statements, and practicing self-care. The chapter highlights the importance of balancing assertiveness with empathy and respect for others.

13

Chapter 13: Cultivating Gratitude

Gratitude is a powerful tool for enhancing well-being and fostering positive relationships. This chapter explores the science of gratitude and its benefits for mental health, physical health, and social well-being. By cultivating gratitude, we can develop a positive mindset and improve our overall quality of life.

Gratitude involves recognizing and appreciating the positive aspects of life. This chapter discusses the psychological and physiological benefits of gratitude, such as increased happiness, reduced stress, and improved immune function. It explores the concept of gratitude as a practice, offering practical tips for developing a gratitude mindset, such as keeping a gratitude journal, writing thank-you notes, and practicing gratitude meditation.

Gratitude can also enhance relationships by fostering positive interactions and building connection. This chapter examines the role of gratitude in social interactions, such as expressing appreciation for others, acknowledging acts of kindness, and cultivating a sense of reciprocity. It provides guidance on incorporating gratitude into daily interactions and creating a culture of appreciation.

The chapter also explores the broader impact of gratitude on society. It discusses the concept of "paying it forward" and the ripple effect of gratitude, where acts of kindness and appreciation spread throughout the community. Practical tips for creating a more grateful society, such as promoting gratitude in the workplace, schools, and community organizations, are provided.

14

Chapter 14: The Path to Enlightenment

Enlightenment is a journey, not a destination. This chapter discusses the principles of personal growth and self-discovery, offering insights into setting and achieving goals, overcoming obstacles, and embracing change. By pursuing enlightenment, we can achieve a higher state of well-being and fulfillment.

Personal growth involves continuously learning and evolving. This chapter explores the importance of setting goals, developing new skills, and seeking out new experiences. It provides practical tips for setting and achieving personal goals, such as creating a vision board, breaking goals into manageable steps, and celebrating progress. The chapter emphasizes the importance of staying curious and open to new opportunities.

Overcoming obstacles is an essential part of the journey to enlightenment. This chapter discusses common challenges, such as fear, self-doubt, and limiting beliefs, and offers strategies for overcoming them. It explores the role of resilience, perseverance, and mindset in achieving personal growth. Practical tips for managing setbacks, staying motivated, and maintaining a positive attitude are provided.

Embracing change is crucial for personal growth and enlightenment. This chapter examines the benefits of change, such as increased adaptability, new opportunities, and personal transformation. It offers guidance on navigating change, such as developing a growth mindset, practicing self-compassion, and seeking support from others. The chapter highlights the importance of embracing uncertainty and viewing change as an opportunity for growth.

15

Chapter 15: Embracing the Wellness Renaissance

The final chapter ties together the themes of health, wealth, and interpersonal enlightenment. It encourages readers to embrace the wellness renaissance and take proactive steps towards a fulfilling life. By integrating the principles of the wellness journey, we can achieve a higher state of well-being and contribute to a more enlightened world.

Embracing the wellness renaissance involves making conscious choices that prioritize holistic well-being. This chapter discusses the importance of aligning daily habits with wellness goals, such as maintaining a balanced diet, staying active, managing finances, and nurturing relationships. It provides practical tips for creating a wellness-focused lifestyle and staying committed to the journey.

The chapter also explores the role of community and support in achieving wellness. It emphasizes the importance of connecting with others who share similar values and goals, creating a network of encouragement and accountability. Practical tips for building and participating in wellness communities, such as joining support groups, attending workshops, and engaging in social activities, are provided.

Finally, the chapter offers a vision of a world where holistic wellness is prioritized and individuals are empowered to achieve their full potential.

It discusses the broader impact of the wellness renaissance on society, such as improved public health, increased financial stability, and stronger communities. The chapter concludes with a call to action for readers to embark on their own wellness journey and contribute to the wellness renaissance.

Book Description: The Wellness Renaissance: A Journey through Health, Wealth, and Interpersonal Enlightenment

In an age where the pursuit of wellness has become more crucial than ever, "The Wellness Renaissance" guides readers through a transformative journey that intertwines the essential elements of health, financial freedom, and meaningful relationships. This book serves as a comprehensive roadmap to achieving a balanced and fulfilling life.

The journey begins with an awakening, inviting readers to embrace a holistic approach to wellness. The book delves into the foundational pillars of physical well-being, including the importance of nutrition, exercise, and sleep. Practical tips and insights are provided to help readers nourish their bodies and cultivate a healthy lifestyle.

Financial wellness is explored in depth, offering valuable guidance on managing personal finances, building wealth, and achieving financial security. The book emphasizes the significance of financial literacy, smart investments, and sustainable wealth, aligning financial goals with personal values for long-term success.

Interpersonal connections and emotional intelligence are highlighted as key components of overall well-being. Readers will discover the power of empathy, mindful communication, and gratitude in fostering positive relationships and achieving personal growth. Strategies for building strong social networks and nurturing meaningful connections are provided.

"The Wellness Renaissance" culminates in a call to action, encouraging readers to embrace the principles of holistic wellness and contribute to a more enlightened world. By integrating health, wealth, and interpersonal enlightenment, readers are empowered to achieve their full potential and lead a fulfilling life.

Embark on this transformative journey and embrace the wellness

CHAPTER 15: EMBRACING THE WELLNESS RENAISSANCE

renaissance—your path to a balanced, vibrant, and enlightened life awaits.

www.ingramcontent.com/pod-product-compliance
Lightning Source LLC
LaVergne TN
LVHW020741090526
838202LV00057BA/6163